# Introduction

In our busy lives many of us try to find time to make a gift or card for a special friend or family member even though time is against us.

Perhaps it serves a deeply felt need to create things for special people as the effort involved endows the gift with greater significance.

It can enhance the pleasure of giving and the recipient will recognise the thought and care involved.

It should not be a pressure and it might be best to reserve these efforts for special occasions, as once a tradition of hand made card giving has been established it is really difficult to stop and people feel disappointed, so beware, because it could become a chore. Making the gift or wrapping could double the pleasure but also double the trouble!

Gift presentation and wrapping is important and it is often difficult to find appropriate paper or cards for special occasions so it is then that perhaps the time spent searching could be better employed in making them.

It would be unrealistic to expect this to apply to every gift but certainly special occasions can be enriched by the thoughtful application of our design and textile skills

Most embroiderers have UFO's (unfinished objects), pieces of dyed and printed fabric, stitch samples, threads, beads and coloured papers in drawers or cupboards.

This is a wonderful opportunity to recycle them into cards, gifts and wrappings and this booklet is designed to suggest ways of applying a wide bank of sometimes unused skills in a practical way.

In previous books we have used an extensive range of techniques and fabrics that include, bonding, transfer painting, colouring and texturing fabric surfaces, hand and machine stitching etc and this book offers alternative suggestions for using these skills

Gifts, cards and wrappings can take numerous forms but many of the ideas can be both fast and effective. However, basic guidelines on composition and colour balance combined with an emphasis on design within shape are strongly emphasised. The examples are designed to whet the appetite and act as a springboard for your ideas.

## Inspirations

Most cultures feature gifts and giving as part of their traditions. Rites of passage and life's major events have long been occasions for such gifts. Birth, marriage and sometimes death have occasioned the ritual presentation of gifts alongside official celebrations both secular and religious.

The annual giving of Maunday money in a special purse by the Sovereign is one example of an ancient tradition still celebrated.

In some countries special cloths form the basis of the gift presentation. In Japan the presentation of gifts is highly symbolic and accompanied by exquisite presentation. The 'fukusa' is an embroidered cloth used in ritual gift giving and can afford wonderful design inspiration.

Rumals are Indian cloths that were also used as part of ritual and ceremonial.

Korean wrapping cloths have featured in several exhibitions i recent years and are spectacula in their colour, pattern and variety.

*Bonded, stitched and trailed PVA samples were applied to mountboard and then glued to the notebooks. This is an excellent way of recycling stitch or design samples. (JL)*

We can use these celebratory cloths as inspiration for our own "wrapping cloths" if we treat them as pathways for our designs. Why not use cloth instead of paper to enclose a gift.? To an embroiderer a carefully chosen fabric could inspire new work. Perhaps you might look upon the methods in the book not only for gifts and giving but also as stepping stones for stimulating fresh thought processes and new ideas.

# All Square

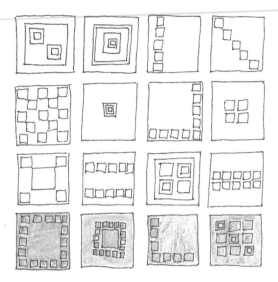

*Thumbnail sketches indicating possible formats for squares*

Knowing where to begin is often the most difficult aspect so a basic shape such as a square or triangle as the design impetus is a simple but effective starting point. The square could be a lifetime theme but small thumbnail sketches exploring line, scale, placing and proportion will indicate broad possibilities. Within minutes several formats will present themselves for a range of possible applications; a set of cushions perhaps or book covers, box tops, brooches etc. Having selected the most promising of the initial sketches they may be further refined, redrawn and coloured or worked in collage.

The sketches could also be developed into paper or fabric patterns in a huge range of techniques, but to gain confidence a limited range of fabrics combined with a' cut and bond 'method yields fast and effective patterns.

The items on these pages have been made from a selected bank of matt and shiny materials in a limited colour range.

• The fabrics were first cut and then ironed onto a piece of 'Bondaweb'

• A grid of squares was drawn onto the backing paper (approximately 2.5 cms or 1")

• The squares of the differing fabrics were cut out and then assembled and recut as required to form variations on a square.

• Care was taken to balance the more vibrant fabrics such as lamé to make sure they did not overwhelm the pattern.

• One fabric in each case was selected to be the main or linking fabric to co-ordinate the various elements.

The resulting designs have been applied to greetings cards, a box top, brooch, and a 'wrapping cloth' seen here used to enclose a gift.

Another square of bonded and stitched fabric has been made into a traditional Japanese construction pulled up with cords into a small bag.

Having worked some simple squares, a set of cards each with a variation on a theme or a group of linked cushions each displaying a different configuration would make lovely gifts.

The cards can be made or bought in packs ready to bond and or stitch and there are many plain card or wooden boxes available for decoration.

The box top was bonded and machine stitched then placed over a piece of cut mount board with 2 oz wadding sandwiched between, then glued to the lid with PVA glue.

*__Right:__ Two book covers with bonded and stitched squares which are simple variations on a theme.*

**Above:** This selection of items using the cut and bond method described includes a box lid, a brooch, hat pins, and a set of cards .They stand on a piece of fabric with a nine square pattern and this could be used for a cushion, bag or a book cover.

**Right:** Based on a pattern of a traditional Japanese bag this lined square has been ,folded and stitched with channels across four corners before inserting the cords which draw it up into a decorative bag.

The two bags featured far right show the wrapping cloth and the Japanese construction drawn into simple traditional bags. (JL)

# Take Heart

**Top:** *The original colour of this velvet box was plain white and designed to be coloured and embellished. Silk paint has given it the base colour and the applique carried out with bonded shapes. This requires baking parchment and careful control of the iron. (JL)*

**Above:** *This set of cards has been printed with variations on a simple heart shape using a foam block and printed with acrylic paint. The iridescent effect was made by trailing a specialised glue designed to accept a printing foil. (JL)*

*The card beneath has also been trailed with PVA glue onto white card and allowed to dry before painting with acrylic paint and burnishing with gold cream.*

As a single unit of pattern the heart is a strong, instantly recognisable dramatic shape with symbolic significance.

The comparatively recent celebration of the Valentine heart on February 14th has given it a visual prominence which can render it over sentimental but that should not deter us as the heart has honourable decorative and symbolic traditions from the mists of time.

The very earliest heart shapes, often fashioned out of precious metal or stone, were a less defined shape and more realistic but over the centuries an exaggerated 'cleavage' has stylised the image and there are many possible explanations for this but the now familiar heart shape is very much part of international culture.

Used in repeating combinations it can make exciting overall patterns or border designs.

Hearts feature in woodcarving throughout Europe and in Poland in particular.

Welsh loving spoons are based on intertwined hearts and foliage.

Hearts have also been woven, printed and stitched into textiles. We can use these traditional images as a source for our own designs.

Bearing in mind how important it is to design within shape, hearts have a universality about them which allows a great deal of leeway as long as we take account of the importance of background spaces, proportion and scale in the design process.

**Right:**
*The background textured paper was printed with orange acrylic paint. The positive and negative printing blocks here were simply made with a string block and 'sculptafoam'.*

*This material changes shape when heat is applied and baking parchment was placed over the foam block and an iron set to wool held on it to heat through for a few seconds.*

*The string heart was then pressed firmly onto the freshly heated block for a few seconds to form the negative block. This is an excellent medium for creating printing blocks and heat can change them back into a flat surface for further shapes if desired.*

*The gift bag was also created from printed textured paper that was bonded and machined before being made up. The pattern was printed with a heart shape cut from foam sponge. (JL)*

**Below:**
*A small cut bonded and machine stitched square can look effective on a simple white card. (JL)*

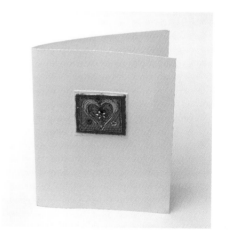

# Silver Threads

*These little cards would be suitable to celebrate a Silver Wedding Anniversary. Discarded machined stitched fabric was used as a ground cloth for bonded applique, Tiny fragments of fabric, thread and various glitter powders were bonded under pieces of sheer nylon scarf. Some French knots and seeding stitches added a dimensional quality. (JB)*

Always challenging and inspiring, a silver colour scheme can be fun to work with. The lustrous greyish white colour can be used most effectively within stitched pictures or hangings. The glint of silver within a waterfall or seascape, frost silvered trees, crystals of ice, champagne bubbles or sunshine glinting on leaves and grasses may suggest the addition of carefully considered hand or machined threads. Any picture whether inspired by the patterns of tubs of flowers on a patio, tree clad hills or the geometric shapes of modern tower blocks can be open to interpretation in any colour but a silvery scheme may introduce another mood suitable for the piece in mind.

As mentioned previously, twenty five years of marriage is celebrated by a Silver Wedding Anniversary. Special cards, small tokens or jewellery all made in silver or including silver coloured elements are given to commemorate the occasion.

Within the fashion world, metallic and beaded surface decoration is associated with glamour. Interestingly, a substantial number of people prefer and feel more comfortable with the colour of silver rather than gold.

The tiniest hint of silver or crystal can upgrade or change the function of a garment or accessory from day to evening wear or from casual to special, or glamorous.

Department stores and specialist cloth stores offer a good selection of silver coloured materials. Some are subtly sumptuous while others can be too shiny and overwhelming for certain projects. You may prefer to colour your own fabric with a wonderful range of fabric paints, acrylics, glitter glues and mediums now available. They are easy to use in the home. Generally non toxic, they are water mixable and may need to be heat fixed by iron.

Having coloured your background material, snippets of silvery fabrics, threads and glitter can be bonded under very sheer fabrics such as polyester chiffon (cheap scarves) or fine nets to enhance the surface further (see Book 3) before any additional stitching.

Fine, medium, thick, corded, faceted, twisted threads and braids can be purchased from specialist suppliers and are tempting to use. Many are made with hints of other colours included so extending the colour range. Machine thread manufacturers provide exciting products too.

All of these tantalising products are in the market place so allow yourself time to play and experiment with some of these suggestions. Enjoy creating splendid surfaces that could be eminently suitable for a number of special items.

The triangular head scarf was created by sandwiching lots of left over machine threads between two layers of soluble fabric. These threads were machined in place by random lines of stitching worked in shaded and silver threads. A more formal patterning was machined on top. A simple edging stitch was worked before the whole piece was placed in water several times to wash away the soluble material. A final rinse in fabric conditioner gave the texture required. The beads were added afterwards. (JB)

The brooch, pin and bracelet were also worked on soluble fabric. The brooch was beaded with crystal beads before the dissolving process. The bracelet has single Sorbello stitches worked in layers to give the stud effect. It was lined with a silver gauze ribbon. (JB)

# "All that glitters..."

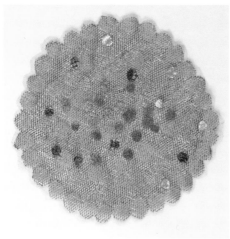

Gold has a universal appeal and radiates warmth and opulence. It has symbolic significance but can be very seductive.

Gold may be sumptuous and brash or subtle and understated. Evocative titles such as 'Field of the cloth of Gold' can act as inspiration.

Research into faded and peeling icons and frescoes will offer a wealth of ideas for unique surfaces.

In heraldry gold and yellow were interchangeable and violet is the complementary colour to yellow. This can be used to good effect when selecting a colour to set off the gold to the best advantage. The tonal value of the violet should reflect the brightness of the gold for really stunning effects.

A Golden Wedding is an anniversary to treasure and could be an opportunity to use gold in profusion. Almost any subject could be rendered in gold. A golden garden for example would provide opportunities for some of the huge range of golds now available.

As with the silver on the previous page, gold is to be found extensively so care should be taken to find the appropriate medium for the task.

Dull yellow, old gold, copper gold, tarnished black gold through to bright and brash could give a huge tonal palette for almost any imagery.

There are countless inks, paints, powders, burnishing creams, guttas, foils and paint sprays which can be used to create luscious metallic surfaces.

Particular care should be taken in the application of gold media as the surfaces can look spotty and ill considered unless carried out sensitively and it is usually advisable to first do a test piece.

**Top:** *This delicate bonded and stitched bag incorporates net, gold lace, lamé and pearls with a contrasting violet net lining. When bonding delicate nets take care not to burn or scorch the net and use baking parchment to avoid sticking problems. (JL)*

**Above:** *The circular bonded coin bag has also been lined with a delicate purple net. It has been left unstitched but could be further developed with delicate hand or machine stitching. (JL)*

Many people find it difficult to present money in a celebratory way. A decorative alternative to the cheque or notes could be an enticing little gold 'sack' of one or two pound coins.

The focus is then placed on the act of giving and the thoughtfulness of the gift. The little bag or sack will act as a permanent reminder of a special occasion. (see above)

The same could be done with silver coins in a silver bag.
The background fabric of transfer painted synthetic velvet has been stencilled with acrylic gold paint through a large plastic stencil.
The antique looking book cover has also been made with transfer painted synthetic velvet as a base. Painted 'Bondaweb' was then applied (see book 3) and

printing foil ironed over very gently and using an iron set to wool heat. This is an excellent method of creating distressed 'iconic' surfaces.
Further detailing was added with a soldering tool to fuse the fibres together.(A respiratory mask should always be worn for this process).
The resulting gilded but stretchy fabric was stretched over stiff

card sandwiching 1oz wadding between the two before being stretched and glued over the card. When dry the stiff paper zigzag and the ribbons were glued to the cover.
The aged looking bag has been worked on black discharge cotton with a bonding and gilding method described in book 3.

# Strips & Stripes

Throughout the ages, stripes of pattern, colour and texture have been included in designs for every type of art medium. Borders painted on ceramic pots, carvings to decorate a church doorway or beading on garments often exploit the versatility of striped arrangements of shapes.

If you focus your observation, objects that surround you in every day life are placed in such a manner. Vertical and horizontal banding of tree bark, the arrangements of fruit and vegetables in your supermarket, rows of crops in a field, or pot plants in a garden centre could suggest a number of creative paths to follow. Varying bands of sand, sea and sky or rows of vibrant coloured tulips may suggest fresh colour schemes to consider.

Whether seen initially as a vertical or horizontal view you are free to change the emphasis as you wish. For instance, horizontal bands of poppies growing in a meadow or fields of lavender and sunflowers can be repositioned as a vertical pattern or reassembled into areas of diagonal stripes or a haphazard arrangement. The representative view would be lost but the essence retained. Motifs taken out of context and re-sited within stripes and showing variations of scale often result in pleasing designs (see Book 5).

Another approach to consider would be to use self-coloured material woven with fine ridges or with thin stripes of colour.

Basic shapes of lines, squares and rectangles can be applied in a line formation ensuring that the fabric pieces are placed on the ground cloth reversing or interchanging the direction of the grain. Understated but interesting effects are likely to emerge.

Shot fabrics are woven in two colours, the warp in one and the weft in the other. Usually worked in shiny fibres, the colour of the material changes when viewed from different positions. Shot silks and polyester taffeta are usually available but are easier to find if featuring in current fashion trends. Applying shapes of the same fabric in varying arrangements on the ground cloth will result in subtle changes of colour and tone.

*Top left: The ends of two scarves are displayed here. The grey one shows simple appliqué shapes where the ridges of the fabric have been turned to give a tonal variation. The blue grey one exploits the contrasting placement of the narrow stripes. They could have been worked in shot taffetas as shown at the top of the photograph. (JB)*

*Left: Patterned machine stitches can be used quite simply to good effect. For this linen waistcoat a matching colour thread was used to echo the lines in the warp and weft and interrupt the surface to create an understated pattern. Self coloured machine enriched fabrics could have numerous applications as wearables for those who would like embellishments that are not overwhelming. (JL)*

*Right: A light mauve synthetic velvet transfer painted with fern prints and resists makes a colourful scarf length. The contrasting strips of polyester satin have been bonded on before being overprinted and machined to secure. (JL)*

*Scarves are a wonderful gift and there are numerous ways of colouring and patterning them in our previous books.*

# Flowers as Tokens

Little bags are always appealing and have been for many centuries. Embroiderers appreciate the finely stitched purses created in Tudor times, the fancy work of the Victorian era, the beaded ones of the 1920's, as well as the variety of styles being created today.

Other cultures around the world have also shown a continual fascination in these intimate items. The beautifully stitched and mirrored bags from the Indian continent, the exquisite silk work from China or the porcupine quills decorating North American Indian pouches illustrate this point.

Beads, shells, feathers and bottle tops are only some of the unusual materials that have been incorporated in the production of these attractive pieces. Many of these longstanding techniques are still being practised and working a small project such as a little bag or neck purse is a delightful way of learning a particular method without having to undertake an epic piece.

The fascination of making a small item to hold a precious token is timeless, It is only the choice of technique and range of materials available that has radically changed. Small is beautiful but working small scale can present problems. Without care, finishing the edges of tiny fabric shapes to prevent fraying, as well as the joinings and fastenings can look clumsy and spoil the desired effect.

Soluble fabric is a comparatively recent addition to the embroiderer's material store. Machine stitching interlinking shapes on this material enables non fraying, delicate shapes to be constructed. As long as an undermesh has been stitched and all the shapes are connected, the motifs or textural stitching should retain their shape when the soluble fabric is washed away with hot or cold water depending on the type of material used (See Book 1)

The little bags illustrated have been inspired by Alpine or rockery plants. Your local garden centre will have a good range to choose from and many of the plants will present the right size with attractive colours and markings. They could well inform a number of other projects you may have in mind.

*Right: The little neck purses illustrated were inspired by alpine plants. Phlox and various types of London Pride. Aubretia was the design source for the neck purse and hair slide shown on the right. The main body of each purse was created by incorporating threads and fabric snippets with machine stitches on soluble cloth before the flowers were sewn in place. Simple stitch networks underpinned the straight stitches of each little flower. Machined cords were made for the straps.*

*The choker was inspired by delicate coloured Dianthus flowers JB.*

Australian landscapes full of colourful wild flowers inspired the little purses illustrated. During a sight seeing trip, quick colour sketches were made using aquarelle crayons to capture the general layout, atmosphere and colour combinations seen.

Machine embroidery on soluble material, incorporating fabric and thread fragments in the working process resulted in a new cloth being created. The rectangular shaped fabric was stitched remembering to turn part of the design to facilitate the front flap. The placing of the straps and fastenings are quite unusual as shown by the trial Vilene mock up. Abstract shapes, stripes, floral motifs and other patterns could be considered too.

*Left:* *These little bags were made by machine stitching on to soluble material to create a new cloth. (see book 1). The paper mock up was made to determine size, colour and position of the design on the front flap. Layers of machine stitch can cause some some shrinkage so be aware that the original size planned may alter a little. (JB)*

*The vilene mockup shown above illustrates how the straps and fastening are placed before the side seams are sewn together.(JB)*

The grey mineral was machined on soluble fabric with purple, grey and silver threads to form a new cloth. Layers of single Romanian couching were placed centrally with some wrapping and beading to embellish.

'Fools gold (iron pyrites) was the design source for this piece. A fine network of stitches was machined on soluble material before layers of Sorbello stitch, wrapping and beading was handstitched on top to give the encrusted effect.

An amethyst inspired this brooch. A new fabric was created before layers of straight stitches were worked over rolled strips of fabric used for padding. Further stitching, wrapping and beading were added. Dimensional paints and glitter glue were incorporated within the stitches to link and encrust. (JB)

# Rocks & Minerals

Rocks and minerals offer a wonderful source for design. The colours, textures, patterning and dimensional qualities are exceptionally appealing to embroiderers. Fabric paints, sheer fabrics, bonded surfaces, metallic threads and layered stitchery can all be considered when interpreting many of the surfaces. The aim should be to capture the essence of the source material rather than attempting a truly literal image. It is usually advisable to select a section out of context rather than allow the outer shape of the fragment or stone to dominate. Simple uncluttered edges are usually best. Small scale embroideries are a good way of building a range of samples exploiting stitched encrusted surfaces. These pieces could be used to make brooches, small bags, box tops or feature on a special card.

Rocks, minerals and precious metals feature on Birthdays and some Wedding Anniversaries. In Astrology each birth sign has a corresponding birthstone. Leos are associated with a tiger eye, Cancer a moonstone and so on. Silver to celebrate 25 years of marriage, gold for 50, and diamond for 60 could be another train of thought, giving wonderful scope for exploiting metallic surfaces. Pearl and rubies represent thirty and forty years respectively.
The possibilities are exciting and challenging. Cards, jewellery, book marks or little books are all containable in size and not too labour intensive and would be most suitable to commemorate these occasions.

**Left:** The three brooches were inspired by semi- precious stones.

**Right:** Various rocks and stones provided the design source for the following stitched samples.

A. The iridescent ridges of a carborundum stone provided the idea for this sample. Layers of fused beads using synthetic materials were couched in place to capture the essence of the surface.(see book 3)

B. Single open chain stitches layered and worked in a square format in a variety of grey and silver give an interesting result. Some of the layered stitches have been wrapped to stabilize. Bonded snippets of silver were trapped under sheer fabric for the ground cloth.

C. A bonded surface incorporating snippets of metallic fabrics and glitter powders provided the background for this interpretation. Blocks of straight stitches were worked haphazardly, some over other stitches for dimensional effect.

D. This sample was worked entirely in raised stem band stitch. Long, short and layered blocks provided the dimensional surface which was encrusted with tiny beads.

E. The clustered knobbly surface of 'fools gold' was initially worked in layers of Sorbello stitch on a ground cloth painted with Gold Mica Flake Acrylic. 'Xpandaprint' or puff paint was applied on and around some of the stitches. Heat was applied by a hair dryer to expand the substance. It was painted with gold fabric paint and tiny beads were sewn in some areas for further texture.

F. Bonded snippets on to 'Tyvek' result in this gently creviced effect after heat was applied. Looped French knots and seeding stitches emphasise the surface giving a glint of gold. (JB)

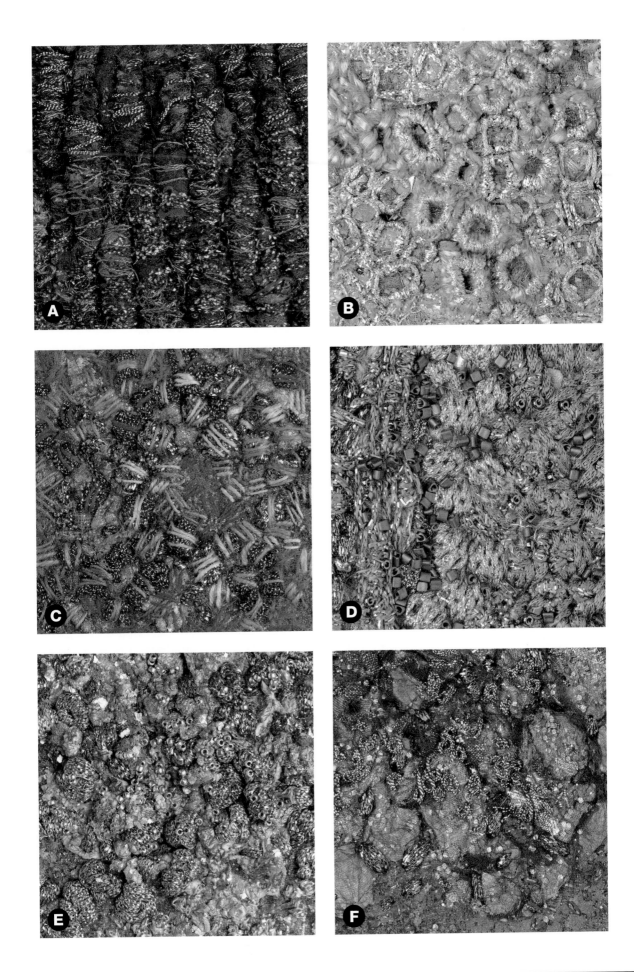

# Celebration Time

*This beautiful head dress was made by Gwen Hedley for the Wedding of her daughter Sarah (now Sarah Hedley-Naidoo). It has been constructed on a metallic head band using assorted pearl beads threaded wrapped and bound into a most effective decorative piece for a very special occasion.*

Most of the items shown here are worked on or include machine embroidery worked on soluble fabric to create machined lace. The delicate effects, non-fraying edges and the beading completed before the background material is washed away enable attractive projects with dainty additions to be made (see Book 1). Lace fabric made this way could also be incorporated into yokes or edges of christening robes as well as dresses for younger bridesmaids. Hat bands and trims could be considered too. Personally customising these pieces would make them even more special. The same effects worked in darker colours and metallics would be eminently suitable for glamorous evening events.

Families have always enjoyed the big events, such as special birthdays, christenings and in particular weddings. Traditionally it's a day of giving. As well as the main presents for the bride and groom, gifts are often presented to the bride from her mother, the bridesmaids from the best man and so on. The presents are a token of affection and one to treasure for a memorable occasion. Many brides also heed the rhyme "something borrowed, something blue".

Wedding days aim to be joyous with the main people and their guests wanting to dress attractively with the bride and bridesmaids looking pretty. The dresses, posies and accessories are usually designed to compliment each other, the occasion and the surroundings.

There is much scope for creative stitchers to contribute. Tiaras, veils and alternative head gear can be decorated with hand and machine stitchery, beads and other additions. The strip design for a bracelet, choker or Alice band could also be adapted to make a daintily exquisite garter. Those of you who prefer working in a bolder technique may like to design and make a prayer cushion or kneeler for the special day. Tiny beads and pearls could add a subtle glint or be heavily encrusted. The design source for the flowers could reflect the bride's preferences. Alpine flowers or delicate blossom could be very suitable. If floral motifs are not desired, equally attractive tracery patterns could be inspired by wood, tile patterns or stone carving found in the building where the event is being held. 'Something blue' can easily be incorporated to maintain the tradition. Most people would love to receive a unique accessory that has been designed especially for them.

***Right:*** *The little bracelet, choker and bag were all worked by machining on to soluble material. For easier working, the little flowers, some handstitching and beaded edges were sewn before the soluble fabric was washed away. The Alice band purchased from a shop was first covered with gathered strips of fine net. The individual flowers were made by the same method as above and applied separately some with beads to embellish the surface further JB*

# ...and more celebrations

This is the golden opportunity to cast off the restraint that may prevent you from using some of the more overt and dazzling techniques at your disposal.

We frequently remind students not to be seduced by the ever growing array of products and techniques available unless they further the integrity of the idea. This could be the time for using them in an explosion of colour and texture to celebrate a particularly special occasion. Many of the 'forbidden fruits' such as feathers , glitter granules, tassels, decorative ribbons and braids as well as beads may be incorporated in special gift wraps and presentation envelopes.
But, when using a profusion of sumptuous materials in this way it may be even more necessary to exercise control over tonal values and placing.

## Boxes

Beautifully embroidered boxes have a long tradition and would of course make wonderful gifts. There are books that give excellent instructions for traditional box making techniques.
It is however possible to customise boxes from around the home as well as bought boxes. These serve the dual purpose of enclosing the gift and as a container for special items afterwards.
The outside can be textured or patterned in various ways. Stitched and applied embroidery may be attached on 'tiles' of various shapes and sizes.
With boxes the greatest care should be taken with the overall shape of the box and the colour and proportion of the decorative additions.
The inside of the box can also be padded using traditional techniques and incorporating fabrics which have been coloured and treated in a range of ways.

## Bags

Bags of all shapes and sizes are available for gifts and the simplest way to construct your own is to carefully deconstruct a bought bag and use it as a pattern.
Paper bags need reinforcing to take the weight of the present and these can all be worked out having taken one shop bought bag apart.
Fabric bags can also be made in this way and stitch or surface embellishment worked on them before being made up. The fabric will need to be supported with some kind of stiffening and 'Vilene' ,felt or hand made paper could be used.
Particular care should be taken with the handles as these can make or break the final look.

There are many ways of constructing fabric bags ,with or without gussets that can be both simple and effective.
Decorated square or rectangular bags are to be found in profusion in the shops and they are easily made and an excellent way of using dyed or stitched samples or UFO's.
Afterwards they could be very useful for carrying jewellery when travelling or for storing special things at home.

**Far left:** This selection of square or rectangular bags all feature velvet which is a voluptuous fabric and highly approropriate for special occasions.

The techniques include bonding, transfer painting and devore (See book 2 for details of techniques).

Two of the bags have been stamp printed with wooden blocks and this is a simple but effective technique for a variety of synthetic or viscose velvets (but not cotton).
A wooden printing block was placed on a flat surface and the velvet placed pile side down onto it. Water was then sprayed onto the back of the velvet and baking parchment placed over it before pressing with a hot iron until the water evaporates. At this point the pattern should be printed into the pile. Always test the heat first as synthetics could melt if the heat is too fierce.

The distressed gilded squares are bonded synthetic velvet with painted 'Bondaweb' and gilding followed by a layer of chiffon which was textured with a heat embossing tool. The gold highlights have been applied with specialised glue and gold transfer foil. (JL)

**Left:** A cardboard box approximately 10cms (4") was the staring point for this 'flight of fancy'. The whole box was painted with a layer of PVA glue and tissue paper applied and smoothed out into gentle textured wrinkles before being painted with iridescent acrylic paints.

A circular piece of card with coloured lace stretched over wadding for a domed effect was stuck to the lid and extensive manipulation of further lace and beads and sequins completed the ornate texture. (JL)

**Right:** The tote bag has been constructed from a transfer painted sheer fabric bonded onto hand made paper. Additional machine stitching has emphasised the design.

A cylindrical poster box forms the basis for an extravagant bonded box with iridescent metallic shards and twinkle glitters bonded under a sheer synthetic nylon. (see book 3)

These highly decorative containers could be used for a range celebratory occasions.

The very extrovert feathered bag has been made from the same bonded fabric finished with strip sequins and a delicate net visible lining as a quiet contrast. (JL)

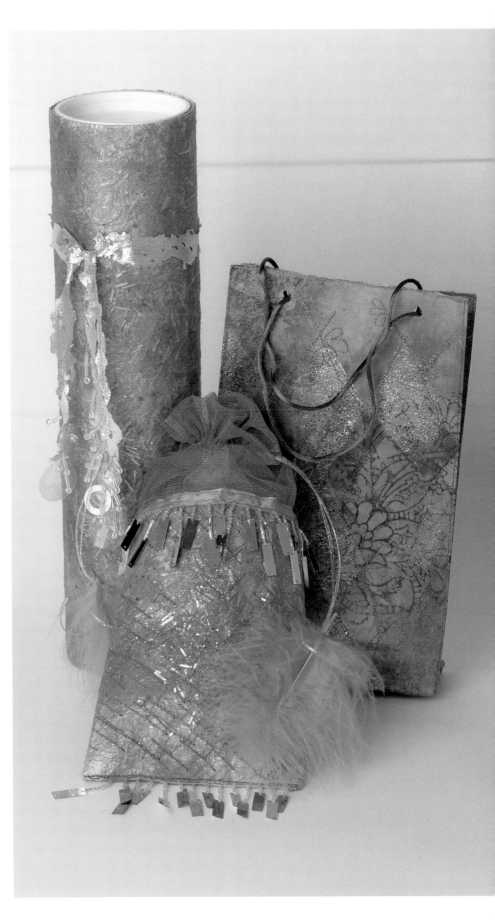

# It's a wrap...

Wrapping a present can be a chore but it is much more interesting if you can customise it for a memorable occasion. The papers or fabrics can be painted, sponged or sprayed as quickly as searching the shops and the result usually more satisfying.
To receive a present thoughtfully wrapped enhances the gift.

## Papers & Cloths

Simple methods can often be the most effective.
Printing or stencilling covers large areas relatively quickly and to good effect.
The papers and cloths seen here have been printed with acrylic surface paints through stencils or with printing blocks either home made or shop bought.
There are some sturdy and excellent stencils available at present and from a most unlikely source.
Horses rumps are often patterned for special presentation and the stencils can be bought from specialist suppliers in a variety of geometric shapes.

*Above:* The tags are an excellent way of using up all sorts of scraps and samples to enrich the art of giving. (JL)

Craft shops have extensive ranges of stencils since this technique has gained in popularity.
A stencil brush is a very good investment and when stencilling make sure the ink or paint is not too watery as it will seep under the stencil and spoil the pattern.
Of course you can make your own stencils and there are special card or plastic sheets available from art shops for the purpose. Should you cut a template or stencil from plain card it is wise to paint it back and front with PVA glue to make it stronger and last longer.
Foam sponge used in upholstery can be cut into shapes quite easily and makes excellent printing blocks.
There are many brands of spray paint available in metallic and non-metallic finishes and some really interesting sprays which give a web like finish.
Always wear a mask when using sprays and work in a well-ventilated space or outside.

## Ribbons & Tags

Although these are often the last things on the list ribbons and braids can be the highlight of the presentation and afterwards the ribbons could be used for simple jewellery such as chokers or hat bands. Tags can be made from almost anything and are a wonderful way of using up special scraps of fabric or paper and even small stitch samples. They can be stitched and personalised or plain and understated. They may also be encrusted and jewel like for extra impact.

## A themed approach

As an alternative to the commercial designs available try working a thematic approach to wrapping. Stars are an obvious symbol but they are universal motifs and found in most cultures either individually or as repeating units.
A colour limit can help and although some of the background papers on this page are handmade some wonderful results can be achieved on brown wrapping paper or with overprinted recycled papers, tissue and crepe papers etc.
String can be sprayed and ribbons and braids constructed and assembled to make extra special gifts.
Other themes could be worked in the same way. A familiar symbol does not have to be a cliché if you approach it in one of the ways described in this book.

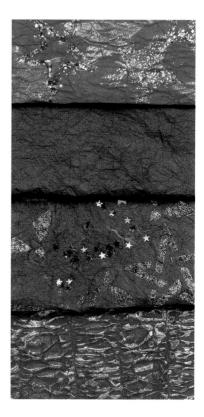

**Above:**
A selection of wrapped parcels. (JL)

**Left:** An assortment of dyed and stencilled papers in a related colour or theme of stars. The textured paper at the bottom incorporates the use of an iron and wax technique. This requires a textured paper and almost any scrunched up paper will be fine. It works best with metallic gold, silver or bronze wax crayons on a medium to dark colour.

Using a flat, NON STEAM iron, melt the crayon on the base of the heated iron and iron over the textured surface where the wax will form seductive patterns. When complete the remaining wax should come off on paper towel and leave the iron unaffected. (JL)

**Right:** The padded lid and lining on the inside of this decorated and painted cigar box features dyed silk sprayed with a specialised gold 'webbing spray'. It contains ribbons and tags and interesting feathers, bells, strings and braids to enhance gifts. The techniques on the ties and ribbons include bonding, beading and transfer painting (polyester ribbon) (JL)

# Postscript

Every aspect of present giving offers opportunities for embellishment.

Envelopes can be plain or decorated and customised with a particular motif or date. Fabric stamps could also contain a symbol or message. Should a cheque be the gift then what better to give it a more celebratory feel than to proffer it in a very special envelope. For the template of the overall shape simply unpick an envelope of the appropriate proportions and use it as a pattern.

Special occasion letters could be written on uniquely designed paper using a variety of printing methods. A set of printed letter papers could also make an unusual gift. (See below)

This book is number 8 in the series and we have enjoyed thinking of some practical applications for the techniques described in previous books along with new ideas. It also offers opportunities to further develop design and stitch skills . Even though some of the materials mentioned could be described as 'gimmicks' unless thoughtfully applied we feel that if the guidelines on spacial awareness, tonal values and designing within shape are adhered to then some beautiful gifts and cards could be made.

Giving is a means of sharing and making the items in the book has given us great pleasure. We hope that you will share that pleasure when developing even more innovative ideas of your own.

**Double Trouble Enterprises**

Booklets in this series include:
1 - Vanishing Act
2 - Voluptuous Velvet
3 - Bonding & Beyond
4 - Transfer to Transform
5 - Gardens & More
6 - Conversations with Constance
7 - Trees as a Theme
8 - Giving Pleasure

For further information or to order please visit our website, www.doubletrouble-ent.com

**Right:** *An assortment of dyed and stencilled papers in a related colour or theme of stars. (JL)*